MW01169519

Reflection With Crow

Lisa Creech Bledsoe

More poetry & other wild things at
AppalachianGround.com

Praise for *Appalachian Ground*

"Author Lisa Creech Bledsoe brings together the natural world of the Appalachian mountains, autobiography and life lessons in a book rich in imagery and wisdom. From meditations to help empty your mind to simple appreciation of the color brown, from lessons learned as a beekeeper and theologian, Bledsoe's words are a gift in an age where we don't stop to look at wildflowers near enough, where beauty has faded to gray in stress-filled times. I am looking forward to her next volume. In the meantime, I will read a poem each night as a lullaby and meditation." —Sis Steele

"This book is a tribute to all things Appalachian. Don't miss taking this mountain adventure with the author. She takes you along with her and the animals through the woods on simple adventures that turn into much, much more. Very enjoyable and heartwarming." —K.M.R.

"Shades of Mary Oliver, Rumi, Emerson, Hemingway and Rilke echo through the sacred hills and valleys of Bledsoe's writing. Some lines hit with the punch of a bare-knuckled boxer, others dance softly like a mountain stream in autumn. Lisa writes from a depth of hard-carved experience, sketching open the very corners of human existence with her words. Read her words and let the mountains call you home to yourself. You won't regret it." —Titanium

Praise for *Wolf Laundry*

"You will settle into her words and stories much the way you imagine she settles into the song of her woods and the lyrics of her bees. There is room in the writing to find your own shared experience, to taste the weather on the mountain, to see imagery that is both clean and deep, like the cool creeks and offering pools she is regularly gifting with attention. Some poems will want you to revisit them, their secrets unyielding until you are ready to hear. Some will welcome you in and share a cup and a cookie with you. Her first collection was great and I gifted it to many, I'll be doing the same with this one. You deserve this. Get it." —Crystal Robbins

"In her first book, *Appalachian Ground*, Lisa Creech Bledsoe gave us love poems to her mountain. In *Wolf Laundry*, she describes what the mountain gives to her — the bees, the crows, the owl; its companionship, its peace, its lessons of hope and endurance. Read the poems for what they teach, or read them for the sheer beauty of the language. "You are this shining bowl, beloved / in your robe of fen and flame." Read the poems." —J. Blackburn

Table of Contents

Reflection With Crow

Here's what the mountain said to me when I arrived:
Try not to wreck this beyond recovery.

That was Crow of course, and it is the nature of
Crow to speak so. Not untruthfully, but certainly
with a sideways cant, which rather ironically matches
the slow undoing in my brain.

Few speak with the mountain without first leaving
something significant behind. In my case, I brought
my significant along in my head, and slowly I am
beginning to understand it.

Or it's understanding me.

Crow brays when I talk about this, turns sidewise
and quivers, a small black joke between us.
I don't mind. Teachers are what they are.

The weather is appalling. I'm in a ragged gray hoodie
and have forgotten my gloves. Crow has a few sardonic
things to declare about my attire; I gaze up, sigh;
my breath gusts out in a long cloud. Crow flutters
and lifts, drifts to a taller tree in mock grievance.

I lean against the Singing Tree in the blowing snow
to weather Crow's intermittent commentaries. It helps
to approach such a one with a wry sense of crooked,
a bit of personal asymmetry or coarseness.

Grist for both our mills.

Long after the Singing Tree's first life, she leaned
to fall, and was caught (willing or not) by the trees
around her. Now she runs aslant, brought by hard wind
to music where her bark scrapes against the others.

Crow watches me listen and shiver. This is what comes
of visiting with Crow. The mountain shows us a
reflection.

Smiling, frozen, I shake and head for home.

Crow and I Discuss Nyx

"One might wonder how such a large and not-so-distant structure remained unnoticed." — Daniel Pomarède, on the discovery of a dwarf galaxy hidden in the center of the Milky Way

Holding to Crow, I begin
to turn. We are stacked like hymnals,
spiraling up through autocrats
and epidemics, galactic dust
and woolen heaps of lemurs dying.

A half-lit coin of moon reveals: You belong
in us, and we in you, bound by the holes
in your wings, hawks in pursuit
and the passageways mice make
beneath rainbent grasses. Still

there are galaxies we cannot see.

I see my reflection
in the gold moon of your eye—
there is no contention between us.
Or when there is, the story conjures
a shade beneath the crow-sown trees,
come to release us to find our lives
before our deaths. We are at once strong

and in peril. It is well to say little,
listen more. None of us will
contend with pulsars or planets
who will have the next and next
and last blazing perfect words
built of light-years and epochs.

Nocturne

"After the collision, the final remnant black hole emits a signal with a constant pitch and decaying amplitude." —*Juan Calderón Bustillo, Galician Institute for High Energy Physics*

A newborn black hole is the shape of a bird.

I mention my conclusion to Crow, who blinks and shifts
weight, wings spilling the color of October cloud.

Not every mystery asks to be solved.

Such are the nature of Crow's missives—I rarely
see them, but there are ripples. The universe creates
itself from nothing and the paperwork is endless.

Black holes collide and a satellite with every color
wings away. I'm inventing the light of course, why not?

It's the remnant, singing, that arouses my interest,
or possibly the uncertainty. There's comfort

in some kinds of information loss as we fall toward
opening. Agreements mean less than the sound of

a great hued bell being struck.

You Are Here

In which I explain to Crow, and am given a story

1. Belonging words

    I'll try to make sense of belonging to words.
    I come from a long line of daredevils
    and clever nomads who knew how to
    get the best of a trade and hightail it out
    before the law got wind. I belonged
    to a lot of broken bones
    back when all the casts were white
    then gray. I was insanely lucky.
    Shag carpet and silver-flecked Formica,
    linoleum outgassing machined security and
    place promises.

    I got a cheap silver necklace from a booth
    at the fair, mesmerized by barkers
    and flashing lights, drugged on the incense
    of candy, asphalt, and carny grime.
    We didn't have a moon and didn't need one.
    I clutched my cheap silver cross in dread of
    vampires while my mother ran the wash at night,
    untangling smaller horrors.
    I assembled fraught altars of words—
    barred the window with them, but
    could still hear a warlike marching music
    each time I turned my ear to the damp pillow.

2. Curvature and stars

    Cradletree swings, sings

nightsong
some chicks gone but day's end
wind rises, calls. We belong
to weightless

The curve returns, we
find our roost under
silver-ribbon clouds—
windspill, beak forward
then jig, hitch and settle
all shadow fade, hush-ahh-shh

It's Spring So We're Both Amiable

Spiritual alchemy, I tell Crow.
That's what makes humans unique.
We can turn darkness into light.

The new ramps are like small rabbit ears
quivering everywhere in the greening slough,
making sharp alchemy of their own.

It's not the same, I say,
watching Crow sidewise while pulling
my boots out of sucking mud. That's
physical alchemy. Science.

Crow becomes shade, and is found by sun again.

We're tricky, I add. Just not uniquely so.
I'd swear Crow grins but
the truth is I'm being ignored.
Tolerated, so long as I don't pull any
loud blunders or stupid shit. Ha, I cackle,
as if I were prone to anything else.
Light into darkness on a regular schedule.

Still, that's spiritual alchemy
of a sort. Nothing Crow about that, though
it's true we're pinched from the same clay.

I've gleaned rock cress, toothwort, and waterleaf
for my bucket—they'll make a meal later in the day.
Mountain swamp vitamins, making me more mountain,
less mono-agriculture. I receive so much more
than I give.

Crow wings out of the slough toward the open field
in search of beetles, or late winterberries.
I wonder what Crow and I are becoming.

Kōzogami

*A well-made sheet is used more effectively when there are areas of
the paper left unprinted to go hand-in-hand with the artist's work.*

1. Washi

Clean lengths of kōzo are cut and tied in bundles,
pounded, separated, stripped. It is the beginning
of the arduous collapse into beauty.

When it is stacked into vats—I have seen this—
the cooking house steams from every corner
thunderheads of fragrant prayer.

There is still unmaking to accomplish,
cleaning, the searching out
and laboring toward becoming.

2. Woman

Decisions separate themselves into snow
flurries. I peel the tape from my exoskeleton—
a wreckage the mud will annex. Wet

and permeable, I smell potential,
a bit like fox and crushed mint, maybe.
I cut and stack lengths of blue every shade

until I am filled and stretched with light
which will not forget its cobalt,
its sun and pale silver. Now

3. Mountain

these thin birch sticks, scraped and built
fragrant into nests until every
mother flushes with yetborn chicks

clamoring for birth. She will add stems
of bee balm, goldenrod, baling twine.
Whatever stands still unmade by winter.

Our senses are draped in white,
winter-wedding gifts. We are
building heat with every song.

4. Crow

Crow peers inside at this new fiber—
a rosy, intoxicated spray of light
on winter's ice. What febrile beauty

we nurture is a lattice of sunwork,
a gossamer web, mostly empty space.
This is how our relationship is built.

There is nothing to judge. There is
only this durable transparency,
this sturdy bamboo walking stick.

Novelist Disappears in a Strange Way From Her Home

Where to begin. Crow and I are
at the Silent Pool, shifting our feet
and waiting for day.

1. *"a bottle labeled poison lead and opium"*

Pain of betrayal, I suggest. Though
in this case the cure was made of death
by increments. Same, same? Years ago
they gave it to babies—cheaper than gin.

Crow's head tilts away and I see
for a moment every color, winged.
Possibilities. No clear lines, only
the infinite, shimmering. Magic 8 ball
says the bottle wasn't hers, anyway.
Not Agatha's. Nevertheless

Crow's clairvoyance stands.
What else is the hare's bolting
toward freedom but an unfolding of
stories with different pinions or burrows?

2. *"fragments of a torn-up postcard"*

Sunningdale, according to a friend,
was getting on Mrs. Christie's nerves. Haunted.
"Tragic associations were felt," the paper mourned.
I roll my eyes. Everywhere is haunted. Places pass
through us, attach themselves like spiderweb,

then ribbon out behind by thousands.

"My wife and I had no quarrel." Hand buzzer
joke postcard, written in disappearing ink.
I wish I could read the three letters
she left behind. Crow shrugs. Ink doesn't
make truth. Love is more spring water

than honey, more mineralled and essential.
I catch the drift. This is what she meant
by her stony stare—a sheaf of futures
hand-torn and scything away in the gale.

3. *"a woman's fur-lined coat, a box of face powder"*

He was having an affair with a younger woman
so: the Silent Pool, presumed bottomless.
This is never, by the way, a publicity stunt. But it is
why witches eat children, or at least look
formidable, incarnating Moon, Winter, Death.

Crow bends sharpens beak on stone: *hah-shet, hah-shet.*
Faces are remembered, taught to children. But who
knows one coyote from another? They will try to eat
your babies until a bigger healing comes.

Crow is more cynical even than I am, but also
a zealot of love. Black feathers gleam with
violet and green dawn. Fire burning on the lake.
I cross my heart before the downstroke of light.

4. *"the end of the loaf of bread"*

Take, eat, body, body, the grove lilts and murmurs.

I hold a birch twig stripped and fragrant: when
I stir up the spring her water tastes of wintermint.
Here there is branch lettuce and watercress so thick
it has altered the stream's passage. Once

my uncle walked in woods a foot thick with
mast—a harvest is so rich entire forests
sprang up overnight, frothing with vines and briars,
sweet with nuts and letters and sheaves of green
gifts, rising and cascading, our daily bread

at the end. What happens if you eat the whole
world? Crow jawks sharply. Life is deeper than hunger,
than your sucking crust and marrow. You are
being carried. Washed ashore like sea glass every
color, becoming the planet on your way to sky.

5. *"a cardboard box and two children's books"*

"She may be hiding, disguised as a man." She
wasn't, but it's still a good way to story-slip.
Now you see her, now he's wearing a blue wool suit
and driving a Pontiac. His name might be A.A. Milne,
or the male lead billed under Greta Garbo.

She checked in to the Swan Hydro under her husband's
mistress's name. A clue, although the papers printed
"loss of memory," as Mr. Christie proposed.
For once, everyone else wrote Agatha's story,
a story they knew by heart, just not hers.

Crow and I are crossing hot asphalt
and eyeing the shadows roaring by, only
one of us anxious.

How Time Travel Presents a Challenge for Humans

When I have hard days I want to write as if
there are no other choices and nothing
else worthwhile in the world to do.
I mention this, then gaze up at Crow.
I'm not holding a can attached to a string
but I still feel silly, anxious. I puff out
a breath: in for a penny.

Crow closes one glossy eye.
Despite the tide and drift of ages,
holy places endure.

I tip that side to side and look
for a spillage of insight.
Nothing.

Wait. Thirty million years—that's my
thought. That's how long Crow's kind
have been carrying food to ghosts,
speaking the languages of clan and kindred.
Seeding new fields, forests, fables.

My kind? Six million, give or take.
Our stories were minted yesterday
or five minutes ago, comparatively.

Crow peers down at me and I see myself
reflected: no one goes alone? Then I see
that's not it at all.

No other creatures are deep time travelers.
Frequent out-of-now flyers. Consider the
lilies of the field, birds of the air
and all that for example. Yeah: just us
wandering around out there, haunting
the past or future, now and then getting
a loaf or a note from crows.

Too damn much time thinking about dying
and what thousand places I'm not, the
ten thousand things I'm not doing right
this minute
today.

Deep breath, nine more.

Crow stretches one wing, turns to face
the other way. Your power is finite,
but not useless.

I smile finally, and recall my clean
timeworn body to the present.

It's a hard holy day.
I walk up the mountain
and put pen to paper.

Where Blessing Lands

I hear an unsubtle rustling above and feel
Crow's presence settle around me in the chancel
of the broken cherry tree, the buckeye already
beginning to flag the woods with red.

I know better than to spill my guts but
do it anyway, breaking out thoughts like
dry corn milled from the cob and scattered,
eaten. Food/link/story is life even though

we're made of more, you and Crow and I
are made of

What? Rightness—
no less the black locust whose rapid rise,
thorns, and creamy blossoms are drunk
with bees in May, all right & becoming.

To this the heart bears witness:
Crow claims seed/coin/memory
unbound by constructs like theft/credit/regret
moved only by life and gift,
unhidden against the clouds. And
tonight as birds roost in the almost-stillness

of night, Coyote will hunt, listening
to the tongue of beech/mouse/strange,
also hungry and blessed.

Signs that Betelgeuse Might Be On the Verge of Collapse

*"We are citizens of a larger cosmos, and the cosmos intervenes in
our lives—often imperceptibly, but sometimes ferociously." —
Brian Fields, professor of Astronomy and of Physics*

It's a red giant. Big! I add needlessly.
The 3D looks like a bleeding death's head.

Crow drops from the tree and sails
ahead without wingbeats. Wary
of the mud—this slough is full of
sinkholes—I follow undeterred.
What if it explodes, goes supernova?

I worry about ridiculous things.
The fate of spiders, my adjective
obsession, killer cosmic rays.
I prefer these to pandemics
or the legitimacy of elections.
Supernovas, at least, offer
a certain remoteness I can't get
any other way. Six hundred light years
feels like a soft place to rest.

The trees don't worry per se, but
they know the bad shit, the rotten
horoscopes. They breathe the dust of
exploded stars and it leaves deep damage,
like the toxins that have littered up
my brain and make me shake and tilt.

Which makes me sound like a pinball machine
doesn't it? All I need are some outlaws
and busty women, a jumble of lights and bells.
I grin into the rain and squint at the
thunderheads while holding a wet Crataegus
for balance, mindful of the thorns. Out here,
there is nothing resembling justice.
Only equilibrium.

I can't find Crow and now the sucking mud
has hold of my left boot. This is not
a good place to stop moving. I want to
avoid a dire reckoning, but accepting
the shock of enlightenment has helped
me reorient more quickly. I pull free
and the outlaw tips his whiskey my way.
My score rattles up, the busty lady winks.

What is the end of life to a star? Or
is that the wrong question. Orion bragged
he could kill every creature on earth—
which pissed off the wrong woman and now he's
made of supergiants, too massive to live
forever any more. Fifty million years
at the outside, then the trees on blue planets
six hundred light years out are in for bad days,
assuming survivors.

What I don't see can be heard. Crow
calls somewhere past the next ridge, indifferent
to my storm, my damage, my stars. There's
no point in resisting Crow's dispassion.
Old wounds will ache until clarity arrives.

We will go where the universe leads us, and
out here, there is nothing resembling justice.
Only equilibrium.

Some Revelation is at Hand

"We didn't believe it ourselves at first. We took 10 years to confirm through experiments that the animals were really actually living without oxygen." — Roberto Danovaro, deep-sea biologist

1.
What lives in me craves light. I close my eyes
and my arms are almost tree. This is a trick
I've only recently learned. My skin ticks
with sugars, sighs and swells toward sky.

Crow cups the air and mounts up—
the forest takes flight below.

I am working my way up the west ridge to sun,
hard going. The mountain forgives few missteps
and the consequences are dire up here, unwinged.

2.
Deep in the sea, miles beneath waves
lie dead zones of immense pressure, salt,
and airlessness. Also: tiny fringed cups, alive.
Making eggs, molting, tentacled.
A millimeter of lace in the anoxic dark.

Something like these also lived before
our atmosphere filled with oxygen.
Circles complete themselves.

3.
Emerging from woods to the exposed ridge
Crow stands on a branch, back to the light, wings
extended, warming.

I grab the next buckeye sapling and pull myself
one deer trail higher, laboring to breathe.

How fire rises in the lungs! Life labors toward
origin: to branch and flame and breath, or
sulphides and sediment and delicate waving fronds
built for the solace of crushing deeps.

4.
Crow's shadow wavers on the forest floor
crosswhipped with shadows of twigs stripped
bare for winter.

I may never be bird. I study the path to wings
but don't know what comes before. Yet once
we both swam and cleaved to darkness, forsaking air,
unknown to the blessing of sun and thermal, caught
in the widening gyre.

There Are No Oaks In My Name But I Begin in Augury

"Everything in the forest is the forest." —Richard Powers, The Overstory

1.
The trees accept me as they accept Crow
and this fierce sleet—together we are howling

and unhewn, not outsiders or others.
Your body shakes and lurches because your brain

has the same broken pathways as mine. Ours
are the same as this planet's: we have contributed

strip mines, petroleum products and maybe
some poetry. Lucky for us very soon after lightning

strikes, fiddleheads unfurl amid the ash
without sharing their agenda.

2.
Today we are spelled rowan, fir, Crow,
chlorofluoromethane—I don't remember the rest

or if I do I pretend otherwise. These things
have a tendency to go downhill.

I tell Crow we are each other and there is
a sudden raw coughing sound, then Crow drops

scat. This is said to be a good omen.
I startle a winter-still hare with my laughter.

Together we are mountain, we are ozone, predator,
perception, righteous eggs and wishing, axis

of the world. Everyone wants to be a queen or killer
whale, not feed the owl's chicks or be washed and

broken down to carbon and river silt. We set out
toward a story believing everything can be ours

but become beechmast and hazelnuts, the forest's
wedding confetti, decaying. We feed the crawfish
        anyway.

3.
Translating my thoughts into you and tree and Crow,
I fly but take centuries to learn to do it.

Meanwhile our seednames are hawthorn, greenbrier
and the sign of all splendid things. Plants sweeten

their nectar when they hear the wingsong of bees—
trees know this and weave it into the future. Every
        moment

there are untried stories blooming unpredictably
by thousands below us in the heaving soil. I can see

mycorrhizae beginning to nourish your synapses—
we slow to harvest carbon dioxide while Crow preens.

The shadow fingers of spruce reach down the mountain into the snowfield below, rewilding what they touch.

Black Crow Brain Blues: A Little Song for "Hello" & "Goodbye"

Dedicated to my brain disorder, your broken pieces, and all the wide, wild mountain

dis tilted
mis unity
ease this

you fly, I
diverge @junction
     split
as they say (or didn't)

my brain and I don't
agree / con flixt
skipskipskip

needle ontherecord
parting (take) hotflight
con nection, that's it
oh yeah

watch that
     step
side show no-wings
swing wise
shakeitup baby
black and bruise
have mercy

re- re- parture
re pair rock actually
naturally healing
is what I'm after
all together
you, us, + bluesbird

vision & join
mar-ry me
fare feather fettle
may as well!
wellfit knit
            laughter

jetroot bluejive
jazz of crows

I enlisten
            side with
tilting
myself wise-sideup
ways to greet
them

it's aaall good

Acknowledgements

Acknowledgement is made with gratitude to the publications where the following poems originally appeared:

Reflection with Crow, published by Red Fez, July 2020

Crow and I Discuss Nyx, published by Menacing Hedge, October 2020

You Are Here, published by Menacing Hedge, October 2020

How Time Travel is a Challenge for Humans, published by Anti-Heroin Chic, February 2021

There Are No Oaks In My Name But I Begin in Augury, published by A Gathering of Tribes, March 2021

Some Revelation is at Hand, published by As It Ought to Be, April 2021

It's Spring So We're Both Amiable, published by Live Nude Poems, June 2021

Kōzogami, published by Softblow, July 2021

Nocturne, published by Chiron Review, December 2021

Where Blessing Lands, published by Grand Little Things, February 2022

Made in United States
Troutdale, OR
01/27/2025

28345828R00020